STAINTON

An Old Westmorland Parish

Reminiscences of a Local Farmer

by

Peter Wood

Published by Helm Press

Dedicated to
The people of Stainton

Printed by Helm Press
10 Abbey Gardens, Natland, Kendal, Cumbria LA9 7SP
Tel: 015395 61321

First published 2003

Typeset in Minion

ISBN 0 9540497 6 4

Typeset and printed by MTP Media Ltd, The Sidings, Beezon Fields,
Kendal, Cumbria LA9 6BL

Front cover: Early picture of Stainton in the early 1900s
John Marsh Photo Archive
Back cover: Canal boat at Stainton Cross 1930s–40s
Jennie Airey

Contents

Overleaf: Excerpt from 1858 Ordnance Survey Map. *Record Office, Kendal*

Introduction

I was born in Nelson, Lancashire, on 8 June 1928. My father worked in a cotton mill, whilst my mother stayed at home and looked after my brother Roger and me.

When I left school at the age of sixteen I went straight into farm work, spending a year at each farm, increasing my knowledge as I went. The first farm I worked at was at Lothersdale in Yorkshire and years later I worked locally at Larkrigg, then at farms at Grayrigg and Milnthorpe where in 1951 I met my wife, Mary. We moved to Field End Farm, Stainton which we rented to begin with and later bought.

I retired from farming in 1974 and enjoy a variety of interests and hobbies including photography, slide shows, music, computers, video, writing and local history. Mary and I have four of a family, three boys and a girl and ten grandchildren and one great grand-child.

I have been researching about Stainton for a number of years and the late Jim Clark kindly gave me some of the descriptive photographs that you will see as you read the book. I have tried where possible to acknowledge and seek permission for all the photographs that I have used. I have also tried to be as accurate as possible, so please forgive any errors that I may have made along the way.

I would like also like to thank the staff in the Local Studies Section at Kendal Library; the staff at the Record Office, County Hall, Kendal and the great number of local residents for all their help and information. Also to John Marsh for lending me some of his archive photographs.

Last but not least, I wish to thank all the farmers from the North of England who taught a mere 'townie' to love the countryside way of life sixty odd years ago! For without them undoubtedly this book would not have been written.

All it remains now is to let you read on and enjoy the history of the many mills in Stainton and my reminiscences of the area!

Peter Wood
October 2003

Location

The village of Stainton lies approximately five miles to the south of Kendal and is one of five of that name known to me. After working and living in or near Stainton during the last fifty years or so, little has changed from what it had been for possibly hundreds of years to what it is today.

The very name suggests it is old for when the majority of habitations and workplaces were still built of mud, wood and thatch, at the time of the Domesday survey, this was and is mostly built of local stone. Some say it was old when the Romans came and was on their main route via Ambleside to the fort at Water Crook, near Kendal, then along to Natland, through Stainton towards Farleton. The road then split to the east for the onward journey to York or south to Chester and towards London.

The Romans were the best water engineers in the world at that time, there was certainly plenty of scope for capturing the energy of the beck and using it for milling corn and all the other processes which could be produced with water power.

Although so close to Kendal and Milnthorpe, a few years ago you would have been hard pushed to find someone who could point you in the right direction or even tell you how to visit the area, though recently it has become more popular with walkers and artists.

As far as I am aware this is the only Stainton village, to give its name to the Parish, which covers some 1,750 acres of mainly fertile land, which is primarily agricultural. It is split by three north/south roads, which link it to Kendal via Natland or Oxenholme and Kirkby Lonsdale, via Old Town or Crooklands and on the old coach road to Burton-in-Lonsdale. It is also possible to travel across the parish on two east/west roads to Sedgwick and Heversham.

Adjoining parishes are: Preston Richard; Hincaster; Sedgwick; Natland; Oxenholme; New Hutton and Old Hutton.

Left: Jim Clark feeding sheep at Stainton Hall on 31 January 1945.
J. H. Cookson, Kendal/late Jim Clark

The area is watered and drained for the most part by the St. Sunday's Beck, which has been renamed Stainton Beck in the village itself. The Kendal/Lancaster Canal crosses the narrow westerly end of the parish and a short section of the West Coast Mainline Railway, clips the south western boundary for a few hundred yards.

Mills

People will be surprised today to find that there were once six prosperous mills in and around Stainton in early the nineteenth century and was an important centre of industry. A few of the mill buildings are still left together with signs of dams and tail races along the beck. There is no sign of a large population ever having lived here so they must have travelled in from the outlying district to work in the many mills.

Viver mill on the south western boundary was believed to have been used by first the Romans and later by monks from a nearby abbey though there is no direct evidence. In John Somervell's book 'Water Power Mills of South Westmorland' (published in 1930) he mentions this as coming under the parish of Hincaster and indeed because of the proximity of the parish boundary, Viver Mill is often described by persons as being in Hincaster or Stainton. At one time Heversham parish covered the whole area and reached certainly as far as Stainton Cross. Ordnance Survey Maps after 1858 show the boundary line going along the lane and down the middle of the tail race but many historical records show it as Hincaster. (The names of the five mills that are carved on the millennium cross were taken from the Domesday survey when Viver was in Hincaster and therefore not mentioned.)

Let us now continue with the history of the mill. The heavy roof timbers probably indicate that it was first thatched before being later heightened and altered to take a slate roof. Originally it got its water supply for the wheel from a shallow lake to the north, which according to Somervell were once fishponds. The old race was visible until the Link Road was built, though for the latter part of its life the

Viver Mill in a dilapidated state.

Tunnel to the flax mill. *Jennie Airey*

supply was taken from a dam across Stainton Beck, just below Bridge End Farm. Basically a corn and maltster mill, it was in use until the 1950s when the dam was washed away and not replaced. He lists the many millers over the last one hundred and seventy years with some familiar local names e.g. Hayhurst, Frear and Wilson. The mill has now been converted into housing and is now split away from the farm that it was originally paired with.

Other water mills in the parish, certainly towards the end of the 1800s were, firstly a flax mill at Stainton Cross. This was separated from Stainton itself by the building of the canal and was about twenty yards from the canal slopes on the southwest side. When the canal was built, they made a tunnel (canal aqueduct) that carries both the beck and a walkway for the mill workers and packhorses to shorten their route.

The old row (weavers cottages) near Stainton Chapel, taken in the 1950s. Looking on are Mrs Jones, Mrs Bateson and Mrs King. They were later demolished and four modern bungalows were built.

Flax or linen was then the main fibre used for outer and under clothing; twine for fishing nets; boot and shoe making; laces and some papers. It was a very versatile material. The seed was used for oil for many purposes and the residue from that process for cattle feed. The mechanisation of the cotton industry in the 1870s spelt the end of the linen industry and the mill that had been run for a time by Robert Caton was taken down in 1886. The stone was then cleared and carried via the tunnel and used to build two of the row of five Stainton Cross cottages on the eastern side of the canal.

I recently had sight of the deeds, conveyances and indentures relating to the mill, that give an interesting insight into a mortgage taken out to purchase the mill and how through default it was sold at the Kings Arms Hotel, Kendal in 1851 for the sum of £755 to a Robert Kendall. Many properties in the 1800s were bought as investments and rented out.

Stainton Mill was the woollen mill situated near the beck just above the village and was run by the Gott's in the eighteenth century. They used to spin yarn that they sold to the well-known Kendal houses of Wilsons, Braithwaites, Ireland and Edmondsons. The weaving had been carried out in six cottages (on the opposite side of the road down towards the chapel) that had been designed to take the handlooms. Later a weaving shed was built opposite the mill. (The mill was eventually knocked down and the stone used for other buildings). Carpets and horse cloth was also made. Machinery was later dismantled and sold to John Fawcett, at Milnthorpe, as scrap iron. The mill was later used for a spell as a bobbin mill and in 1925 because of its dangerous state was taken down.

The mill cottages had a small well in their back garden and all their rubbish went into the beck. The houses were small, dark and cold. Yet Mr King, the chapel caretaker for many years, was born and lived all his 60/70 years there. The small gardens at the front were always well kept. Eventually the residents were re-housed in Milnthorpe and Grayrigg and the building demolished to make way for the bungalows.

Next we come to Low Bridge Mill at Skettlegill (originally Scuttlegill) where there is still evidence of the ancient millrace and old mill still standing. This had always been a bobbin mill until around 1860. Somervell states that the house was said to have been an inn at one time and was on the busy packhorse route to the port of Milnthorpe and that the old stables had doorways at one time wide enough to take a packhorse fully laden – though there is no evidence of this today.

The corn and maltster mill at Mill Bridge on the A65 had a twenty-two foot iron wheel, with four stones, a rolling mill and a circular saw, producing amongst others sawn or kibbled oats. It worked until 1958 and converted in 1969 to a house that is currently run as a guest house.

The highest mill on the beck is at Halfpenny and this has had a very chequered history being involved in the manufacture of flax, dye, manure, paper, cocoa matting, comb and sugar boiling. It was knocked down and the stone was reused in other buildings.

In Somervell's book he lists the above five (six including Viver) water mills and their importance and lastly finishes of with an interesting mill at High House where silk top hats were made. In addition to this there may in fact have been yet another mill bringing the total to eight. There is a shallow depression across the field lying between the village and Stainton Cross which is probably all that remains of the race for another ancient mill, though there has been nothing written about this.

So it can be seen that with the proliferation of mills Stainton was certainly a busy and thriving place.

Home Produce and Markets

The majority of the original houses had their own plot of land to grow a little food or produce a commodity, which could, by bartering or exchanging, help to keep the small community almost self-contained. Though there is some evidence that some essentials were shipped into Milnthorpe and reached this area by horse and cart.

Eventually as the population outside the area required more food and clothing, the mills were put to good use for grinding oatmeal and a little flour for the home and other grain for animal feed. With Kendal flourishing as one of the main market towns (Burton-in-Kendal was the main agricultural market for many years) eggs, bacon, cheese, butter and the occasional knitted socks were traded there. Butter was churned for sale and home consumption and great blocks of salt and saltpetre bought in for curing the bacon and ham. Rabbits were snared for extra meat to supplement the cheese that most farms made.

I can remember the occupier of Steps End walking to Kendal twice a week with her basket of butter and produce on her arm and returning with goods for the house. Steps End in the early part of last century (20th) had its own slaughterhouse and the meat from there was transported round the local area in a horse and trap. In the early 1980s whilst clearing some land adjacent, near the riverside, a large quantity of coins were found, ranging from Henry VIII to Charles II. This was treasure trove and a special coroner's court was held. The court concluded that the coins were the nest egg of a wealthy 17th century mill owner. The only other known find at an earlier date was a rusty broadsword in the beck also found by children playing.

Farmers

Horses were the main source of power for the farms, though some of the smaller holdings had their farm lad to help with the work. If animals couldn't be sold locally they were walked to Kendal or Milnthorpe to be sold at the market. Often the smaller stock was carried in the cart. In more modern times motorised vehicles were used and wagons often carried stock from two or three farms in the locality.

Ploughing with single furrow plough at Stainton Hall in January 1941.
J. H. Cookson, Kendal/late Jim Clark

Two Clydesdale horses harnessed for ploughing with Jim Clark. *late Jim Clark*

Tommy Newhouse and Ronnie Swanton farm workers at Bridge End in the summer of 1948 with Fordson tractor loaded with corn sheaves.
Alice (nee Taylor) Sadler

I can remember when the electric prodder came out in the 1960s, a device which administered a substantial shock to any animal that was being obstinate. On one occasion some unruly bullocks were being loaded on at Bridge End bridge and when one was prodded for refusing to go up the ramp into the wagon, it jumped over the wall and into the beck. Fortunately it was no worse for the experience.

Family farms would often call on grand parents, aunts, uncles and children to help at the busy times of the year. In the hayfield there was turning and cocking and shaking out, all labour intensive hand-work. Many of the meadows and cornfields would be mown with scythes* and sickles. Any root crops grown were labour intensive and I, along with others, can remember tying sacks round my knees and crawling along the rows and rows of turnips, carrots and kale to thin them to a respectable distance for ten pennies or a shilling (5p) for a hundred yards. Some farmers used hoes to knock out the unwanted clumps and then went through the ones which were left a few weeks later to single them. Most of the weeds that grew were removed with a horse drawn side hoe, locally called a scurrifier or scuffler and was also used for other root crops.

On the small acreage field the grass would be ploughed with a one or two horse plough, harrowed with a spiked wooden frame then lifted into ridges with a special ridging plough. Some farmers preferred to spread manure on the land before ploughing. Others spread it directly into the furrows and then the sprouted seed potatoes were planted by hand, after which the ridging plough split the ridges back to cover them.

*

* The six foot English scythe was standard farm equipment. Usually sharpened on the hand turned sandstone wheel in the yard and kept sharp by stroking it with a strickle, a flat piece of wood which was dipped in tar and covered with sand. Later the introduction of the smaller American scythe and sand stone or later carborundum whetstones commonly called, 'bullstones' became the easier option.

Weeds

Weeding the common dock was a back breaking, hand staining, straining job. Mowing nettles and thistles had to be done with a scythe. The large sow or scotch thistles were usually stubbed out individually. Also in root crops, charlock or wild mustard, which could and did survive under grass as dormant seeds for over a hundred years, was covered with minute hairs, which played havoc with skin when pulling out.

Most weeds were left in the furrows to rot down or be hoed in but horse tail/mares tail and ragwort were pulled and burnt. Ragwort because it killed stock that ate it and horsetail because it caused violent diarrhoea (scouring) if eaten, even dried in hay. There were others but these are the ones I have had experience of. If there was a large amount of couch or wick grass it was often carted off the ploughing and composted with layers of lime then spread some years later when it had rotted down.

Remedies

Walking round the parish and looking at the plants it's possible to work out some of the remedies that the locals used before 'modern medicines' came into being. Nearly every community had someone they could turn to in the event of illness or accident. Here are just a few of the plants that were used:

- Comfrey: was one of the main plants used for sprains, strains and bruising. The root mixed with sugar was also taken for a horrible complaint in the 17th century called 'whites'.
- Foxgloves: very poisonous, but recommended to be taken only by those of a strong constitution for rheumatism.
- Leek: grown and used for asthma, coughs and lung complaints.
- Greater celandine: jaundice, scurvy and sore eyes.

Right: Ted Clarke (left) having a natter with an unknown local farmer on a winter's morning in the 1940s on Stainton Lane, near Skettlegill.
J. H. Cookson, Kendal/late Jim Clark

· Lesser celandine: piles.
· Scarlet pimpernel: small pox, measles and to bring on a sweat.
· Garlic: for cleaning the blood.
· Herb Robert: to stop bleeding.
· Crab apple: for sore mouths.
· Couch grass seeds (a handful): for the common headache.

Many of the orchards have disappeared but apples, pears, damsons and other soft fruits such as raspberries that were good against sickness - gooseberries and currants can still be seen.

My mother made a medicine to ease a bad stomach from rhubarb and bicarbonate of soda.

A common cure for insect bites and small sores, bruising and sprains, is just coming back into fashion as distilled Witch Hazel and its modern derivations.

This of course is just a small sample of some of the plants and flowers used.

But back to the farming.

Crofters

Many of the people in the area were a type of crofter. That is people who made a living from two or three ventures. They lived in a cottage with a few square yards of land to keep a cow or a goat for milk and a pig for either bacon or breeding for sucklers; a sheep or two for the wool and to keep the grass down; a few hens or ducks for eggs and possibly a goose or two towards Christmas and to provide that invaluable commodity goose grease, which they coated themselves with under their clothes to keep the cold out from November to April.

'Ne'er cast a clout till the May is out' referred to the blossom of the May tree (hawthorn to you and me). This also resulted in June being the month for weddings as many people took off the goose greased clothes they had worn all winter in May.

Back Lane, Stainton taken in the 1960s. On the right is Rose Hill with the Meeting House (now gone) just behind. On the left is the barn belonging to Dreamlands Farm.

More often than not there would only be one or two bulls kept in the parish and many farmers walked cows to them. Similarly with boars, sometimes in an adjoining parish, though usually there would be more than one tup.

The majority of working horses were geldings or mares so again sires were itinerant and possibly served many parishes. Working dogs for sheep and cattle were expensive and not as plentiful as in later years. Horses were the main power source used for the parish field work with ploughs, harrows, carts and so on and the width of many of the lanes reflects that even today. Some farms had a horse gin to drive grinders, pump water and threshers before steam power was available in the early 1900s, when steam traction engines took over. Bullocks and horses had been used for hundreds of years for this, as well as milling corn, crushing grapes etc. The animal is hitched to a long pole attached to a central post and walks round. As it turns the power is transferred either by cogs, or belt and pulley to the machine it has to drive.

With the coming of the canal in the early 1800s the ease of transporting the rural produce to the larger towns and thence to the ports, began the change from isolated semi-self sufficient communities to a trading and interchange of goods from other areas and abroad. One of the main commodities shipped into the parish was coal, which replaced some of the wood and peat, most of which came from the mosses on each side of the Kent estuary. The easy way of stoking the open fire was to feed a longish branch into the flames and keep moving it up. This of course required someone to sit in the easy chair by the fire and keep an eye on it. A good winter job for the older man or woman, or younger apprentice! Tommy Frear ran a taxi service with a horse and trap for many years, taking people to catch the bus at Stainton road end or to the shops at Milnthorpe.

Waybend Cottage, Stainton. This was before it was extended, with the plaque above the door – 'Joseph Whitwell, Grocer Provisions, Dealer and Licensed to sell tobaccos'. Joseph was also sexton, roadman and had the Post Office – a very busy man! Pre First World War the P.O. was marked on the map as being the top one of the two Bromley Cottages. *John Marsh Photo Archive*

Hirings

Men and boys used to be hired at the two fairs in Kendal usually held on the New Road area, when all the farmers wanting staff gathered along with those requiring work. The prospective employers asked questions relating to the experience and quality of work of the labourers and offered a sum of money for the next six months. The labourers would ask for a general outline of the farm and if they were to live in, whether it was a good 'Tommy Shop' and about time off. If an agreement was made then the employer handing the worker a shilling piece (5p) sealed the deal and the bargain was made. If the employee wished to leave after the six months then he handed back the shilling and returned to the hiring to try his luck elsewhere.

Some of the larger farms in the parish used to hire an Irishman for hay time many of whom were excellent workers. Odd ones refused to do any other jobs if the weather stopped the hay making though they still wanted their hire fee. Most returned to the same farm for a number of years. Many worked in season from the root crop thinning, hay time, harvest, and fruit picking or gathering root crops in different parts of the country. Money was sent home to their families, after expenses at the local of course!

The Home

Talking of home, the houses in the parish were all built of local limestone with a small amount of imported freestone for the flagged floors and slate for the roofs. The majority before the 1950s still had stone sinks in which to wash up, with water brought from the well or in some cases out of the beck. Stainton Cross had a hand pump between the old barn and the row of houses. When it dried up the occupants walked under the aqueduct to where the flax mill used to be and took water from a spring there. Bridge End at one time had a wind pump behind the Dutch barn and in later years after it had gone, water was pumped from the wellspring near the beck with a stationary diesel engine. When that dried up they too carried it from the spring by the site of the flax mill.

The iron fire range in the kitchen probably had a side boiler, which had to be filled by hand to heat any water required and one or two ovens on the opposite side. There was often a swinging iron side-grid to boil a kettle or pan. Some of the older models had chains to hang the kettle over the fire.

A few people still remember having to fetch the old tin bath in from its place on the wall in the scullery. Having placed it in front of the fire, usually on the sacking or pegged cloth rug, water was ladled out of the boiler, cooled if necessary with cold water, and with carbolic soap and a scrubbing brush, had their weekly bath. There were occasions when the event was taken in a separate room with no heating and a stone flagged floor, not very nice in the middle of winter! In many cases only the steam on the window stopped curious passers by from watching what was going on inside.

If it was dark the only light was often a couple of candles, a small paraffin lamp or in more modern times, if you were fortunate, a pressure or Aladdin mantle lamp. There are still the remains of the outside toilets to be found at some of the residences. In a parish where there was and is no sewage system they were devised to be the best of the day. Usually a small building either isolated or as part of another, a short way from the house and handy to the farm midden stead. Some were simply a stone base with the seat fixed above it and everything piled up until it was shovelled out. In others the seat was high enough for a bucket to be placed under, usually with a separate small door behind to remove it to the midden or into the muck cart if the midden was being emptied. One I knew was actually a wooden shed built over the top corner of the midden. Ash pits were sometimes next to or behind the toilet and they were cleaned out at the same time. Nothing was wasted and all shippon and stable liquid waste was run into an underground tank, be it built of wood, brick or stone and then pumped out by hand into a special cart and spread on the land. Often, in more modern times, when water closets were installed as upgrades in the living quarters they were connected to the same tank. Most are now connected to septic tanks.

Villagers

In the past, many people rarely moved far away and were often related to each other. Outsiders often made the mistake of making a remark to one particular person only to find they were talking to a cousin, brother/sister-in-law or other relation. Eventually, as the local families lost their heirs, either through accident, wars, marriage, or moved to more productive farms, other families moved in and as time passed the occupants of the village changed. In Stainton the Whitwells, Addisons and Nelsons were long time residents, some dating back to the 1600s. The Whitwell and Addison families had a finger in the building of Stainton Chapel when they broke away from the Church in the 1660s and the Nelsons helped with the replacement church building.

If you look through the records of the surrounding parishes many of the surnames which were in Stainton in the early 1900s can be found. Blacksmiths, farmers, joiners and craftsmen who wanted to improve their living, because there is a limit on how many of these trades a small village can support, moved on to the growing populations of the small towns with more opportunities. Their off-spring through three generations are now in modern jobs.

Farms

A hundred years ago there were farms scattered throughout the parish – Viver and mill, Sellet Hall, Cross Crake, Low, Middle and High Barrows Green, Helm End (Old Hutton), Helm Side, Helm End (Barrows Green), Underhelme, Mill Bridge, High House, Spout House, Cockrigg, Knots, Halfpenny, Scuttlegill or Skettlegill, Stainton Mill, Dreamlands, Stainton Hall, Stainton Cross, Steps End, Croft House and Croft Cottage. These were mostly run by a small family, husband, wife and one or two children. The larger farms would have a farm lad and/or a dairymaid often doubling as a home help as well.

During and just after the war many farms survived thanks to the use of Prisoners of War (POWs) who took the opportunity of getting out into the countryside with its fresh air and in many cases better food and company. Any that were true Nazis and refused to work didn't last much longer than a couple of days before they were told their services were no longer required.

Clothes and rugs were nearly always made on site. During the last war women often had to improvise and make their own clothes. Calf meal bags were fine woven cotton and the farm ladies washed them and made underwear. Aprons were more often than not made from a fine hessian proven bag. After the wars ex-servicemen were introduced into farming and continued the tradition. Wool was washed spun and knitted, old rags were pegged into sacking for rugs and very heavy too. Most areas had their ash or oak swill and basket maker. Fuel was carted from the coppices and peat from the mosses that nearly all parishes had a share in. When the canal opened in 1819, with it came coal and tallow that previously came by ship to Storth or Milnthorpe and had to be carted round the villages that added to the price.

Canal

There are the remains of the wharves at the majority of the villages along the canal. It was used as a supply and transport route until the end of the last war when the Natland to Kendal length was closed and used as the Kendal Corporation rubbish tip and the Stainton/Natland length, closed some ten to twelve years later, with the Link road utilising part of the route in the 1980s

By the late 1940s the fishing in the canal was excellent and coach loads of fishermen from the Wigan area were often spread out along the Stainton/Crooklands stretch competing for the best catch. One weekend one of the bigger coaches attempted to go over the hump bridge at Bridge End and being longer than the older models was straddled across the top. The fishermen had to get out and push to free it and eventually they stopped coming. The canal level was lowered and wagons with large tanks on were filled with the fish that were netted and carted away. Some people said to Wigan Reaches

The bridge at Stainton Cross that the boat pictured below has just passed under. *Jenny Airey*

Canal boat at Stainton Cross in 1930s–40s. *Jennie Airey*

though we never found out for sure. However the canal was partially cleaned out and refilled. Fish barriers were built across in about five places. It turned out that a university was using it as an experiment in weed eating carp. Fishing of any sort was banned for many years. Eventually the fish were removed and the fences taken down. Some fishermen caught some whoppers that had missed being captured.

Many people used the canal as a level walk but that and the fishing was again banned in 2000 when the Foot & Mouth crisis was around. Opened as a linear park the last few years have seen a great increase in pedestrians, cyclists, and horse riders. The grass is periodically mown and the hedges looked after much better and that has saved a great many lost hours by farmers attempting to retrieve stray cattle and sheep.

Talking of the bridge at Bridge End, I once saw an old canvas topped Railton car travelling too fast towards it. As it basically jumped off the top of the crest, a man's head appeared through the

Shyreaks - these council built 'Airey' houses were part of the home building edict in 1947. An extra piece of land had to be bought for a septic tank to service them but electricity and water was connected from the mains. All but one are still rented.

top shouting for the driver to stop. Being inside, it took a few seconds for him to realise what had happened. The argument that followed is best left out. I wish I had had my camera!

Wildlife

Mink that were thought to have found their way from a farm near Bentham played havoc with the wildlife and upwards of a hundred were captured in traps over a few years, both on the canal and in Stainton Beck. Herons from Milnthorpe, swans, kingfishers, mallard and Canada geese have all been seen in the area. As have the general bird population including, great, blue, coal, and long-tail tits, rooks, crows, magpies, owls, sparrow-hawks, kestrels, buzzards, finches, wagtails, robins, wrens, blackbirds, mistle and song thrushes and tree-creepers. The list goes on and yes, there are hedgehogs, foxes, pheasants, hares, deer and in some parts badgers.

Timber, Poultry and Vermin

Timber for building was mostly cut locally or imported from the ship breakers yards, though some of the large estates sold standing oak for ship building and for use in the mines or mills and elm for waterwheels and cartwheels for export. Holly wood was sought after by the watermill owners to make the patterns for casting the iron cogs and collars, required to keep the mill running and before cast iron, for the gears themselves. Sometimes when food was short in a severe winter trees were polled and the branches thrown down for the sheep to chew.

Many housewives kept a few hens, ducks or geese and it was disaster if foxes took them. One fox in a hen house could destroy thirty or forty just for killings sake and probably only take a couple off to eat. Young lambs were also on their menu. Stoats, weasels, magpies and crows took eggs when they could.

Hawthorn Cottage and phone box just before the ford as you enter the village.
The cottage is believed to have been a Roman weigh house.

Rats and mice made their homes in hay and corn stacks and ate their way through wooden doors and into buildings looking for food. The remains of oat and other cereals are still found within the walls of the old buildings.

Lime and Potash Kilns

Lime was a commodity used for mixing the mortar for building and old kilns abound, some specially constructed for use during the building of the canal bridges. (One of the quarries used for this was sited just above the chapel where a house now stands). Others so as to produce a saleable commodity for the land which because of its sandy, gravely, stony nature, leached the calcium away quite quickly. Potash kilns provided the fulling mills with their main commodity.

Modernisation

The new Stainton Hall was converted into two houses and more recently the buildings into six more. The woollen mill house and some of the buildings were also modernised in the late 1900s as were many of the other farms. High and Middle Barrows Green, Helm End and Broom Rigg were all converted to modern housing. The small cottage at Cross Farm was extended into the barn. Steps End was mostly rebuilt and the list goes on, as Bridge End is in the throes of conversion as I write this.

Electricity and Telephone

Mains electricity so often taken for granted nowadays, was only connected to some farms in the 1950s. Previously as dynamos became more plentiful after the war there were many 12, 24 or 110 volt systems codged-up (designed) by enthusiastic inventors, who were tired of trimming wicks and filling paraffin lamps. Wires were often strung up with bare bulbs to provide a little light and anyone with a stationary engine for grinding corn, could connect a generator and a mass of 6 or 12 volt batteries to supply the house. Many wireless sets were still driven by a dry Grid Bias battery and a rechargeable wet battery or accumulator. The original crystal sets had all but disappeared before the war but transistors were still to be invented.

Stainton Hall in the early 1900s. *John Marsh Photo Archive*

Cars and vans were still provided with a starting handle and many old bangers were converted for use on the farms. Fitting an extra gearbox to get slow traction with a decent engine speed, they were used for carting and towing as a cheap alternative to the scarce and much more expensive modern (then) tractors. Roads were not gritted or salted outside the towns and anyone with a motor or steam vehicle always carried chains to be fitted in inclement weather. This was the era when the working horse began to disappear from the land.

If you needed to contact a doctor or anyone urgently there was usually a telephone at the Post Office or occasionally the manor house. Sometimes a public telephone would be put in a wooden box on a pole in the village, so people could call when the PO was closed or arrangements made for people to use one located in a house. Eventually the red telephone boxes were placed in a usable position. Most farms were eventually connected by the mid 1950s.

Hedging, Fencing and Walling

Considering that the parish has a substantial amount of limestone available, it is noticeable that the majority of the field boundaries have been and are formed by hedges. Many of the hedges were planted to provide shelter for stock and fuel when they were laid in a seven-year cycle. Many of the smaller fields have been joined by destroying the dividing hedge and with them have gone a great number of plants, which sustained numerous species of wildlife. But hedges meant work with a capital W. Every year they had to be trimmed with a slashing hook. Usually curved, occasionally straight, the sharpened steel on the end of a longish shaft, had to be wielded by hand to cut back the growth on both sides and the top of the hedge. It took weeks of skilled, muscular work to slash the miles of hedge on a medium sized farm and that wasn't the end of it! With fork and rake it had all to be gathered up and burnt. Each year the

Right: Ted and Jim Clark busy hedge laying at Stainton Hall in January 1941.
J. H. Cookson, Kendal/late Jim Clark

hedge grew it added slightly to the height and width and eventually it was left to grow tall enough to be laid.

This was another skilled and time-consuming job usually attended to in the winter months. The advantage of this was that it provided firewood, all for the cost of trimming it out, with an axe and saw, often done by an older member of the family, and again the seemingly endless cleaning up. If there were sheep to be put in the field the raking had to be thorough. Anyone who has had to catch a sheep and grabbed a handful of thorn clippings will vouch for the pain it provides.

Many hedges were originally planted with hawthorn, blackthorn, ash, hazel, holly, sycamore and the like. Birds added wild rose, blackberry, and other fruit bearing plants. Many hedges were planted on a dyke or banking which had to be negotiated in order to slash or lay the hedge above. Rabbits dug their burrows and sheep and cattle scratched them down. They had to be rebuilt. That's why hedges are WORK but they provided a lot of shelter in inclement weather and are havens for birds and wild life.

On the other hand stonewalls are a good way to get rid of unwanted stones from the ploughing. If they're constructed well they stay up for years without further work and if a gap does fall, it can often be rebuilt in a couple of days.

Barbed wire was the next invention to be used, it was cheapish and with wooden posts saved from the hedges or bought in, could be quickly erected and keep stock in place. Fences built with home-grown wood from hedging and copse, were a more permanent fixture than the old fashioned hurdles but often didn't last very many years. When hedges get old they tend to grow open in the bottoms and sheep can easily escape. So instead of replanting and/or stuffing them with dead thorns because plain wire and then woven sheep netting were becoming both more plentiful and cheaper, hedges were fenced off and allowed to deteriorate. Electric fences are still seen in fields to control grazing and are handy as a stopgap for emergencies. Modern rotary hedge cutters can do in a day what it took many weeks to achieve, with very little clearing up.

Water

One of the main criterias for locating a farm or village in the past must have been to find a constant supply of good fresh water. With most of Stainton Parish on a limestone sub strata there was little difficulty in diviners finding the necessary springs and the beck was an obvious choice as far as stock was concerned. St. Sunday's (Stainton) Beck as already mentioned, was used for driving the waterwheels and to wash away much of the rubbish. Tom Beck on the southern boundary was certainly used as a water supply in much the same way. When Lupton Reservoir was extended from an ancient tarn, its service pipes spread across the surrounding country to include Milnthorpe, Crooklands, Endmoor and Stainton village to name but a few. Because of the distance many outlying farms were not given the privilege of connection and had to maintain their private supply. Some of those that were on the track of the new Manchester pipeline from the Lake District were joined to that. There was a communal pump in the field opposite the Punch Bowl at Barrows Green, until mains was connected but even now in 2003 there are still some properties in the area with their own private supply.

I was told some time ago that there was a boiler/engine manufacturer in Stainton village but have not yet found out where. For a great many years there was an old vertical boiler in use as a water tank at the end of the buildings at Stainton Hall but that could have been imported. Talking of Stainton Hall it's funny how things turn around. The old maps showed the farm buildings alongside the road where the current house is and when that was built about 1887, the original Hall was used as the barn and shippons. That area has now reverted back to housing.

The majority of farmers recognised their animals by their markings, though names such as Buttercup and Daisy were often used for cattle and passed on to the offspring with a number Daisy 1 or 2 etc as the years passed by. A great number of the fields were also named: Long Pasture, Brow Side, White Field and Hardlands. Occasionally if a farmer had settled a debt for some commodity bought by exchanging it for land, it would be named as Smith's Meadow or Clark's Pasture and that often stuck even when the land had been bought back. In 1986/7 there was a survey of field names made by the Women's Institute and a copy of this is held at the Record Office, County Hall, Kendal.

Smoke from the locomotives blown by the prevailing wind was blamed for the frequent rotting of the telephone wires along the Sellet road to school.

Church, Chapel and School

In 1190 there was an ancient chapel at Crosscrake that was a ruin in 1773, when a new church that preceded the present one built in 1874/5 replaced it.

The little chapel in the village was built as a nonconformist place of worship in 1697 by local labour and there was, at one time, a one storey meeting house on the back lane over the packhorse bridge. One elderly lady I spoke to remembers as a girl, going to church in the morning, chapel in the afternoon and the meeting house in the evening.

The school at Crosscrake has been rebuilt and extended in stages throughout its history and is currently being upgraded yet again with a large number of pupils coming in from adjoining parishes. The staff is dedicated and the school as a whole has an excellent record. Over the decades pupils walked to school, cycled and were brought in horse and traps, cars and now buses. As well as the teachers there are a great many parents who give their time and skills to assist in the learning process be it physical, mental or computing.

The population of the parish at the turn of the 1900s was around 300 to 320. Today it is very similar though with new housing and conversions, plus a mainly imported population it would be expected to be more. Perhaps it is due to the closure of the farms and migration of young villagers to the towns through being priced out.

St. Thomas's Church had a tower until it was declared unsafe when it was removed and rebuilt as it is today.

Stainton Chapel in the 1950s, now only used twice a month for worship by the United Reform Church.

Weather Folklore

I have been asked at times about folklore concerning the weather. Much I have learnt as I worked around the country, some peculiar to the parish. Here are a few samples:

- If you can hear the trains on Arnside Viaduct expect rain within 12 hours.
- If you can smell linoleum from Williamsons Factory in Lancaster expect a downpour for two or more days (now closed).
- If the trains rattle above Oxenholme it will be clear and cold.
- If the cat goes wild in the house expect rough weather within 24 hours.
- If the cat sits and washes itself with its back to the fire expect wet weather.
- When birds roost near the ground expect rough weather and similarly if gulls congregate on farm land on a fine afternoon.
- If the scarlet pimpernel flower is seen it will be fine for a short time.
- If you see a mackerel sky – not long wet not long dry.
- Ice in October to bear a duck, the rest of the winter - slush and muck!
- If the new moon cradles the old, fine weather is foretold
- If the moon has a halo around it, rain is in the offing. Count the stars within and add twelve hours for each.
- A halo round the sun close in, signifies wet weather within 24 hours, halo farther away rain in 48 hours.

There are of course many more and associated with many other aspects of life. Many to do with weddings and good and bad luck but I'll not bother you with them here. So I'll finish with one I particularly like – Morning fog and grassy dew brings a day that's fine for you!

Footpaths

If you like walking there are still a few footpaths in the parish which would have originally been made by people travelling to and from Stainton on foot or possibly with a donkey or a pony to get to a place of work, or as a short cut to school or church or whatever. I've already mentioned the canal towpath and there's a short wooded walk along the back banks (opposite side). There's a longer path that travels through the parish from the boundary at Eskrigg Wood via Skettlegill to Sedgwick Bridge. Another one which follows the St. Sunday's Beck for quite a way eastwards from Halfpenny with a branch from High House joining in near Stang Farm.

A Day in the Life of a Mid 20th Century Farmer

Talking of time perhaps a day in the life of a mid 20th century farmer might be interesting. Go back to a time of no mains electricity, no telephone, no mains sewage or water and no gas. It is a dark October morning and the clockwork alarm rings in the day at 5.30am. You rouse, light your candle, get dressed in your working clothes and make your way to the kitchen. First up, you lay the fire in the Yorkist (fireplace) and light it. Once the sticks are burning you put on the coal and fill the heavy iron kettle with cold water from the one tap supplying the sink. Swing the hob over the fire and put the kettle on. If no one else has arrived you have a cold wash at the sink then go into the scullery to light the paraffin lanterns that you need for the morning's chores. Hopefully by this time the boss and the other lad have reached the kitchen. If the fire has burned well the kettle could be boiling though highly unlikely before you've assembled the cooler, the milk kit and the scile (filter), put on your boots or clogs and returned to the kitchen for your morning cuppa'.

The cows in the shippons, mistles or sheds (according to which area you are in) rouse as you enter the door and the dim light from your lantern allows you to find the nail in the beam above to hang it on. You pick up the stiff brush and sweep off the bedding from the vicinity of the cow's feet, take another light into the provender store and return to the dairy for your two-gallon milking bucket. The majority of the cows had names and all their little foibles were known. Back to the provender store for the scoop to measure out the cow's ration into the wooden box (sometimes a galvanised bucket) that was placed for the animal to eat as you milked it. Your copy or three-legged stool was taken from its place and you sat and milked your first cow.

Gascoigne milking machine, 12 gallon steel milk kit and 1 cwt bag of dairy nuts.

The mistles were low and dark but warm and you were so used to the smell of the animals that you never noticed it. The majority of the cattle around this time were Shorthorns, red and white patched, roaned, blue crossed, black polls, Ayrshire, occasionally a Jersey, indeed anything that looked like producing a good quantity of milk. In those days a cow giving around two gallons a day was a good one. When one was milked the milk was carried to the dairy, the bucket lifted above your shoulder height and tipped into the container that held the filter (more often than not a piece of fine cotton cloth) above the cooler. Then repeat the process for the next cow and

Right: Hay time at Bridge End in 1991. By this time there was little hay made but baling with balers like this came in during the 1950s, previously it was carted loose with horses or occasionally swept to a stationary baler which made larger bales fastened with iron wire. A commodity, which found a great many uses on the farm. This type of baler used sisal string and later plastic string. Today they are mostly very large round bales and have to be lifted mechanically.

the next and so on, until all were milked. A good milker could deal with six to eight an hour dependent on the animals.

Depending on the time you expected the milk wagon to arrive, the horse had to be caught from the paddock brought in and geared up to the cart, the kits rolled out and lifted in and taken to the milk stand for collection. Some kits were conical and held sixteen gallons, though twelve-gallon upright kits were becoming more available. They were made of galvanised steel and heavy. The empties, left yesterday, were picked up and taken back to the farm dairy. The cattle were given a feed of hay and the horse tied up ready for further use.

Breakfast often consisted of a bowl of porridge or groats, followed by a typical breakfast of fried bread, egg, bacon, and toast or bread and marmalade and tea. As soon as it was finished it was back outside again to clean out the manure from the shippons, feed any calves, pigs, young stock and generally tidy up the yard. The dairy equipment was washed and swilled out. There was a break for tea and cake or biscuits then the general work of the day could start.

Leading manure into the meadows, heaps seven drags full each, seven yards apart, rows seven yards apart, all as neat as possible to help when you had to go and spread them with a five grain fork. Possibly you'd be putting up a wall gap or slashing a hedge, carting food to or from an out barn, counting sheep, pulling turnips or digging potatoes, cutting kale or cabbage, whatever the weather. Making clamps of mangolds or spuds and if it was really wet, curry combing the cows and the horse, or sawing firewood, or mending fences. Always so much to be done and all by hard work.

Dinnertime was always welcome you'd wash off your footwear and enter the warmth of the kitchen. The table, covered with an old copy of the local paper someone had passed on, held a plate and a mug and the utensils; knife, fork and spoon. Depending on the whims of the farmer's wife you were fed on potatoes, vegetables and

Left: There were many licensed cattle wagon owners willing to take stock to and from the auctions or to farms for so much a head or journey in the 1950s and 1960s. Previously a great number of cattle and sheep were walked to market, sometimes for quite a few miles. Nowadays most farmers transport their own stock.

meat. It was surprising what amount could disappear in five minutes. Pudding was served on the same plate that you had just cleared and was often rice or semolina with jam and cream or perhaps the occasional cake mixture and all swilled down with a substantial quantity of tea. You were lucky to get five minutes after to digest it before going back out to your tasks.

Occasionally if the paraffin was getting low you were sent down to the village store with a gallon tin and perhaps asked to buy cigarettes or tobacco or some other commodity. Your work was still waiting when you returned and still had to be finished by three o'clock when there was another brew before feeding the stock. Sometimes teatime was around 4 or 4.30pm and cheese or jam and bread followed by a slab of cake was the norm. Then it was back to milking, and tidying up. If nothing else was urgent you could retire for the evening often around 8.30 or 9pm for supper that could be hot soup or cake or cold sandwiches with cocoa, tea or milk. The paraffin lamp in the house would be on the table and you could read or help peg a rag rug or some other occupation until you lit your candle and went off to your bedroom.

There were variations, Saturday night you might get away to the pub in the village or catch a bus to the nearest town. There were Young Farmers Clubs beginning to spring up or the church might have an event on. You could stop up all night if a cow was expected to calve or if one was ill and required treatment. In hay time grass was often mown in the early hours before it got too hot for the horses and to save time during the day for other work. Meadows were mown in bits that could be handled reasonably well.

Nowadays the large tractors and modern machines can drop a field in a day that previously took over a week. During the war many grass land farms had to plough old grass and sow cereals and they were helped by the War Ag. (Westmorland War Agricultural), which had a local depot at Oxenholme. Most farmers still had horses and the War Ag. was fully mechanised to help speed up production. The Land Girls (Women's Land Army) were also important at this time working with horses and livestock and helping to sow corn or cultivate and generally help where men had left for the war. Farming was a reserved occupation as far as National Service was concerned, likewise mining. Rationing was still a major problem after the war had ended but extra food coupons could be obtained for threshing days and though the local policeman had to verify any pig killing, there were a few ways (illicit) of keeping the ham and bacon on the table. I remember a story told by my father whereby a mill worker asked the known black marketeer to supply him with a ham for his daughter's wedding. After a littler persuasion he agreed and duly provided the joint. Some months later the seller was complaining to a colleague that he hadn't received any payment. When told who owed him the money and that he was a bad payer, the seller exclaimed, 'If I'd known that I'd have charged him twice as much!'

During the war cattle feed that wasn't home grown was on coupons and rationed. Most was and still is the by-product of food or other house consumables such as margarine and soap etc. In dried cake form came linseed, palm kernel, cottonseed and from the flourmills, bran and thirds (part of the wheat grain). Other feeds bought in were crushed beans and peas and surplus potatoes covered in blue dye as unfit for human consumption. Many farmers washed them and used them in the house. Dried grass was becoming popular and cattle feed manufacturers began to experiment with quality-balanced foods for different types of stock. These were delivered in one hundred weight hessian bags at so much a ton and cut down on a great deal of work for the farmer. Most were fed at 4.5 lbs to a gallon of milk produced and also kept the animals quiet while milking. This was done by hand in most farms until the late 1940s and early 1950s when milking machines became popular.

The Future

From the information that has been available, it appears that the parish of Stainton has had a lively past in the history of the area, providing a great many commodities and services to those that required

A recent photograph of the village showing the packhorse bridge. On the left is Waybend Cottage, then Bridge House and Bridge Cottage, with Beck Side on the right.

them. The little beck with its mills and associated farms is still here in 2003.

What of the future? Well with plans to reopen the canal; to build a new auction mart and re-align the lane leading from Lane Ends to the village; with ideas for the chapel building to be utilised for community use as well as worship; with more farms being converted to housing and horse riding on the rise, the Parish Council is confident that the future looks bright for this picturesque Westmorland village.

The author sitting at the village cross situated on the A65 junction to the village. This was carved by John Marshall of Stainton, from a local oak tree felled in a storm and was erected on 15 December 1999, to commemorate the new millennium.

If you have enjoyed this book you may also enjoy other books published by Helm Press.

'**A Westmorland Shepherd**' His life, poems and songs

'**Elephants On The Line**' Tales of a Cumbrian Railwayman

'**Dear Mr Salvin**' The story of the building of a 19th century Ulverston church

'**All In A Lifetime**' The story of a Dalesman as told to June Fisher

'**Hawkshead Revisited**" A Walk in time through Hawkshead

'**A Century of Heversham and Leasgill**' A walk in time through these old Westmorland villages

'**An Old Westmorland Garage**' The story behind Crabtree's of Kendal

'**Ambleside Remembered**' People and Places, Past and Present

'**Snagging Turnips and Scaling Muck**' The Women's Land Army in Westmorland

'**The Windermere Ferry**' History, Boats, Ferrymen & Passengers

'**Kendal Green**' A Georgian Wasteland Transformed

'**Kendal Brown**' The History of Kendal's Tobacco & Snuff Industry

'**On and Off the Rails** The Life of a Westmorland Railwayman

HELM PRESS
10 Abbey Gardens, Natland, Kendal, Cumbria LA9 7SP
Tel: 015395 61321
E-mail: HelmPress@natland.freeserve.co.uk